CW01572923

EXPLORING
CLOTHES

Brenda Ralph Lewis

Illustrated by Stephen Wheele

Exploring the Past

Editor: Amanda Earl
Series Editor: Stephen Setford
Designed by: Ross George

Cover picture Spectators arriving at Lords Cricket Ground to watch a match between Eton and Harrow in 1937.

First published in 1988 by
Wayland (Publishers) Ltd
61 Western Road, Hove
East Sussex, England BN3 1JD

British Library Cataloguing in Publication Data
Lewis, Brenda Ralph
    Exploring clothes. – (Exploring the past).
    1. Clothing and dress – Juvenile
    literature
    I. Title   II. Series
    646′.3   GT518

    ISBN 1–85210–006–0

Phototypeset by Kalligrahics Ltd, Redhill, Surrey
Printed in Italy by
G. Canale & C.S.p.A., Turin
Bound in the U.K. by The Bath Press, Avon

Contents

1 Exploring clothes

People are the only living creatures on Earth who wear clothes. Unlike creatures who have their own fur, feathers, scales or thick hides, we have only thin, vulnerable skin. So, we must protect ourselves from cold or heat, and from getting wet in rain or snowstorms. Clothes, however, have other purposes, too. They say a great deal about us – where we live, how we live, what kind of climate we live in, what sort of work we do and whether we are rich or poor.

Clothes tell us a great deal about people. What do the clothes worn by the people in this family portrait tell us about their lives and when they lived?

Clothes have always given this information. In addition, the clothes people wore in the past tell us what culture or civilization they belonged to, what century they lived in, and how their home and working lives were different from our own.

Clothes are therefore much more than just something to cover ourselves with. They are full of clues about the people who wore them in the past, and the people who wear them now.

This book aims to give you some of those clues and to help you discover others for yourself. You can do this not only by reading the text, but also by taking part in the many different projects and activities that are outlined in the book.

Clothes today

People today often have different clothes for different purposes. They have clothes for work, such as overalls for working in factories or suits for the office. There are special clothes for parties, casual clothes like jeans and tee-shirts for relaxing, and track suits, swimsuits and other clothes for playing sports. Many people like to follow fashion, and as fashions change quite often, so do their clothes.

The clothes some people wear regularly are traditional ones. Indian women, for instance, traditionally wear *saris,* and although they may have different colours and patterns, the basic style of a *sari* remains the same. It is like this with other traditional clothes, like the wrapover skirts or *sarongs* worn by men and women in Sri Lanka and the Pacific Islands. *Saris* and *sarongs* have been worn for many centuries.

People who do not dress traditionally today have a greater variety of clothing than ever before. They also have greater freedom to dress, if they want to, in a way that expresses their feelings.

Many people still wear traditional clothes. These Muslim girls in London are wearing the Islamic salwar *(trousers) and* kameez *(dress).*

Lots of people like to follow fashion. In the late 1970s, 'punk rock' was very popular.

5

For instance, the punk rockers on page 5 probably dressed like this to rebel against 'conventional' clothes. It was not always like this. People in the past used to keep their finest clothes for parties and other special occasions, and early this century, it was important to have a 'Sunday best' outfit for going to church.

Casual and sports clothes have only been popular in the last fifty years or so. Before that, people played sports in their everyday clothes. If you look at old pictures or postcards of holiday-makers by the sea sixty or seventy years ago, you will see that they wore the same clothes they wore at home. They just did not have any others.

Ask people you know about their clothes, and

Specially designed sports clothes have only been popular for about 50 years. Before this, everyday clothes were worn to play most sports. Can you imagine trying to play tennis in a long skirt like this?

see what clues their answers give you about their lives. You could ask what work they do, and what clothes they wear for work. Do they play sports? If so, what clothes do they have for this purpose? Do they have any special clothes for other activities, like gardening or fishing. Do they do anything that means they must wear protective clothing? You may find they wear protective clothes for working on the car or to protect themselves in dangerous work areas – like radioactive environments.

Next, take a walk in the street of your town, and look at what people are wearing. Record what you see on a chart similar to the one below. You could do this on several days within a month and compare the different types of clothes worn on each day. Do you think you will see the same clothes on a Saturday compared to a weekday?

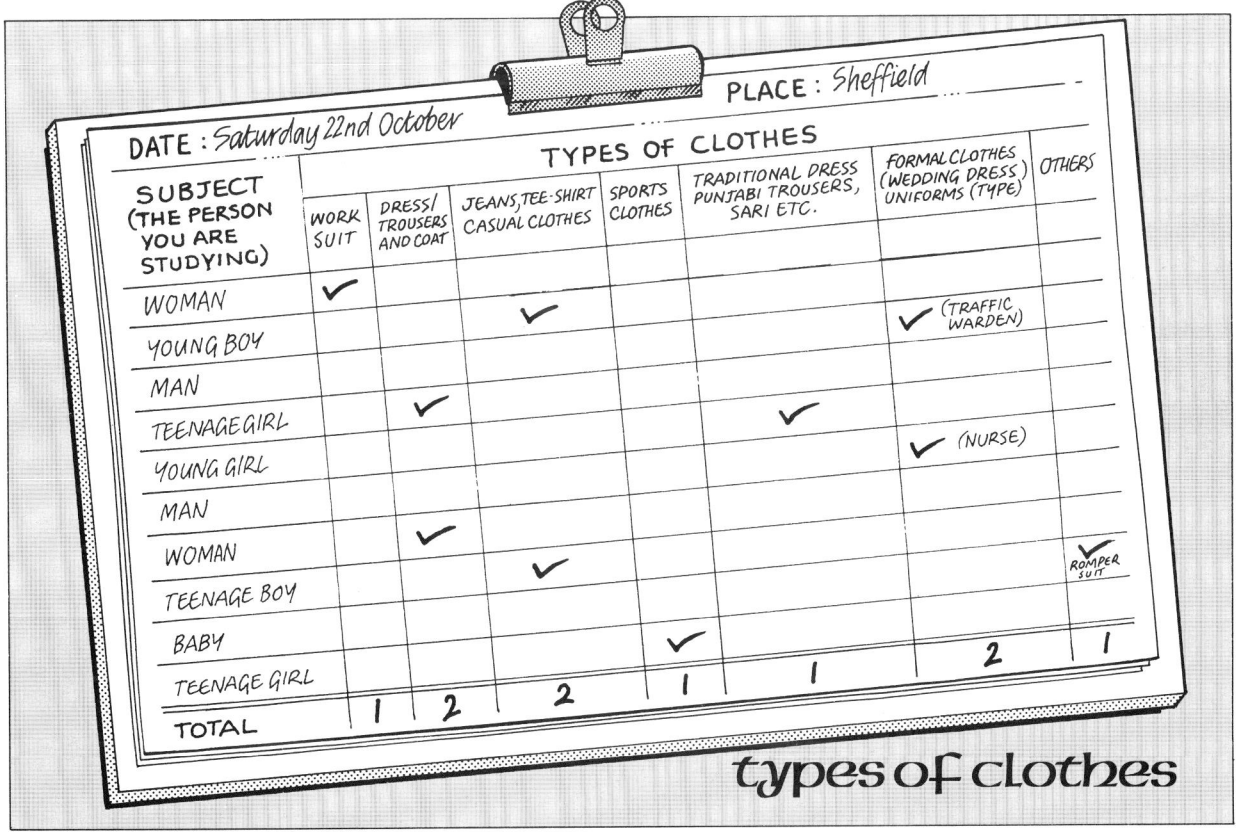

DATE: Saturday 22nd October PLACE: Sheffield

TYPES OF CLOTHES

SUBJECT (THE PERSON YOU ARE STUDYING)	WORK SUIT	DRESS/ TROUSERS AND COAT	JEANS, TEE-SHIRT CASUAL CLOTHES	SPORTS CLOTHES	TRADITIONAL DRESS PUNJABI TROUSERS, SARI ETC.	FORMAL CLOTHES (WEDDING DRESS) UNIFORMS (TYPE)	OTHERS
WOMAN	✓						
YOUNG BOY			✓			✓ (TRAFFIC WARDEN)	
MAN							
TEENAGE GIRL		✓			✓		
YOUNG GIRL						✓ (NURSE)	
MAN							
WOMAN		✓					
TEENAGE BOY			✓				
BABY				✓			✓ ROMPER SUIT
TEENAGE GIRL							
TOTAL	1	2	2	1	1	2	1

types of clothes

Your clothes are made from . . . synthetics

Until about a century ago, the clothes people wore were all made from 'natural fibres' like cotton and flax, which are both taken from plants, or silk, wool and fur. Then, in France in 1889, scientists made viscose-rayon, the first 'synthetic' or artificial material.

Rayon was supposed to be an artificial kind of silk. Natural silk comes from silkworms' larvae, and other natural fibres are grown in fields or taken from animals. Synthetics, however, are chemically-made. Viscose-rayon was made out of cellulose taken from plants or trees. Other synthetics, like nylon, come from chemical mixtures called polymers.

Today, natural fibres are still worn, but since 1950 very large numbers of our clothes have been mass-produced in factories, using synthetics like polyester and acrylic as well as nylon and rayon. Clothes made from these synthetics are often cheaper, and wear very well. They are also easier to wash and keep clean.

Left *Rayon, a synthetic material, being made from cellulose. Rayon was made to resemble natural silk.*

Look at the labels on your clothes and compare them with the labels on this page. List the materials mentioned; for example, polycotton, polyester, acrylic, pure new wool, cotton. Which ones are synthetics? One of the above is a mixture of synthetics and natural fibres. Which one?

Fibres are mixed for several reasons. One is that the synthetic content makes the material last longer. How many other reasons can you think of? Test the qualities of synthetic materials. Wash a piece of nylon or polyester as illustrated on this page. It should dry fairly quickly. Find out why it does so.

Synthetic materials are now part of our everyday lives. Everyone has become used to them. Ask your family and friends why they think synthetic materials are useful for clothes. When buying summer clothes, do people prefer to wear synthetics or natural fibres? Ask them to explain their preference. Note down their answers, and then decide whether synthetics or natural fibres are more popular. Also decide what is the main reason why the 'winner' has come out on top.

Drying times of materials

1. Wash a nylon or polyester garment in a small bowl and wring out the excess water.

2. Time how long it takes to dry the material.
Do the same with a cotton garment and a mixed material garment such as polycotton. How long do they take to dry?

3. Draw a small chart of your findings. What does this tell you?

MATERIAL	TIME TO DRY
NYLON	3/4 HOUR
COTTON	3 HOURS
POLYCOTTON	1½ HOURS

Clothes Labels

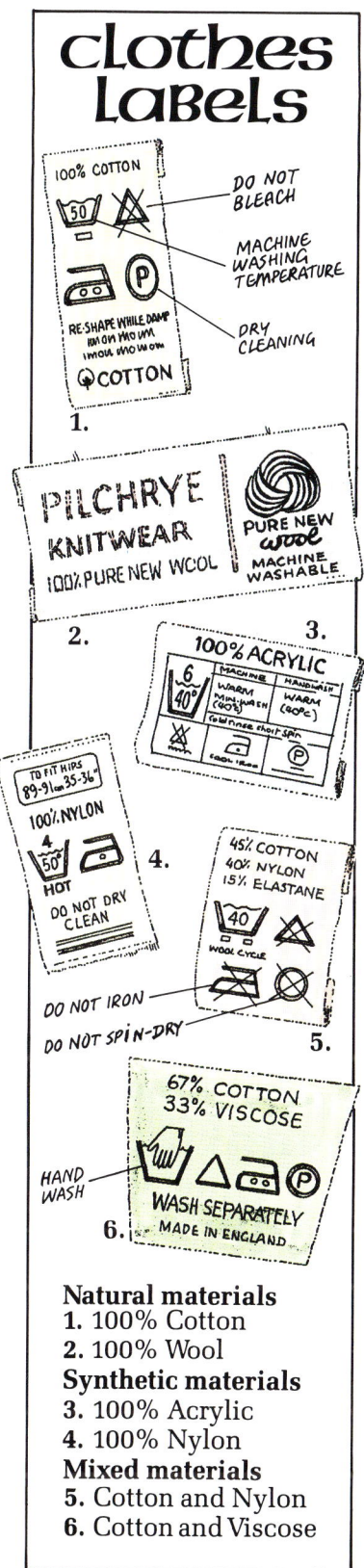

Natural materials
1. 100% Cotton
2. 100% Wool
Synthetic materials
3. 100% Acrylic
4. 100% Nylon
Mixed materials
5. Cotton and Nylon
6. Cotton and Viscose

Your clothes are made from . . . natural fibres

The first 'natural' materials used for clothes were the animal skins worn by prehistoric hunting peoples. They believed the skins of animals they wore would give them the strength and courage of these creatures. People no longer believe this, of course, and today we have hundreds of other materials to wear. Even so, animal skins and furs are still worn by some people, although most people now feel that killing animals for their fur is very cruel. Leather is also obtained from animal hides and silk is from the silkworm larvae.

Other natural materials can be 'grown'. In about 3,000 BC, cotton was being grown in the Indus Valley of India. These cotton plants grew in fields and their fluffy 'flowers' were picked off by hand. These flowers were the raw, or basic, material from which thread was made. Gradually, cotton growing spread to Egypt, Africa and America.

Wool is 'grown' by sheep and by llamas, alpacas and vicuñas in the Andes mountains of South America. These animals have their thick coats sheared or cut off to make into wool. In the past, people were careful not to waste wool, and used to look at the fences round fields to see if the sheep had scraped off any tufts from their coats. These tufts were gathered and used for spinning.

Left Animal skins and furs are still worn by some people, but more and more people now choose to wear warm, practical coats, such as ski-jackets. This nineteenth-century advertisement highlights the cruelty of killing beautiful, wild animals for their fur.

types of materials

NAME	Cardigan Jumper	Skirt Trousers	Blouse Shirt	Shoes, boots Trainers	Coat
Simon	N	m	S	N	m
Sally	m	N	S	S	N
Ranjit	N	S	m	m	N
Sam	S	m	m	S	m
Peter	m	m	N	m	S
Jillie	N	N	m	N	S
Steve	m	N	S	m	m
Camilla	N	m	m	m	m
Gary	S	m	S	N	m
Mandy	S	m	m	S	m

TOTAL: NATURAL MATERIALS = 13   N = NATURAL MATERIALS
SYNTHETIC MATERIALS = 13   S = SYNTHETIC MATERIALS
MIXED MATERIALS = 24   M = MIXED MATERIALS

Left Draw a chart, similar to the one on this page, to show what types of materials are most commonly worn by your classmates.

Look again at the labels on your clothes or school uniform. How much natural fibre are you wearing? Are your shoes made of natural material, such as leather, or from synthetic materials such as plastic? Which of the natural fibres grow in fields and which were taken from animals?

Look at the chart on this page. Together with your classmates, make a chart of your findings for natural fibres, synthetic materials and mixed materials (eg. polycotton, wool and acrylic).

Compare the types of materials. Which is warmer on your skin? Which one is lighter in weight? Which kind of material is more stretchable? Which one needs more ironing than the other, and why? A lot of people think it is wrong to kill animals for clothing materials. What do you think? Suppose there was a law to stop this happening. What other materials could we easily use for coats, gloves and shoes?

2 How clothes are made

From fibres to cloth

Until about two centuries ago, the work of turning fibres into cloth was done by hand, with the help of simple machines. The distaffs, spindles and spinning wheel in the picture were used to spin fibres into long 'strings'. These strings were wound into balls. Then, the fibre was woven into cloth on machines called looms. Looms wove by looping rows of horizontal (side to side) fibres into rows of vertical (up and down) fibres. Fibres like wool can be looped and knotted into jumpers or cardigans on knitting needles.

Until the late eighteenth century in Britain, cloth was woven by workers in their own homes. This changed when big machines were built to spin and weave cloth in factories. The introduction of machines to do work formerly done by hand is known as the Industrial Revolution, which started in Britain in the early 1750s. Factory machines worked more quickly, and so produced more cloth.

Communities of workers and their families often grew up around the mills and factories. Are there any old mills in or near the place where you live? If you have a local history society in your area (find out about this at your local library) ask the members what they know about the old mill. What was made there? When did the mill close down? Who worked there and where did they live?

With a strong magnifying glass, look at a piece of woven cloth, such as tartan, to see how it was made. How many colours can you see in it?

Above Until the late eighteenth century, wool fibres were spun into thread on simple spinning wheels, similar to the one above.

Below After spinning, the wool threads were woven into cloth, similar to this picture.

how to weave cloth

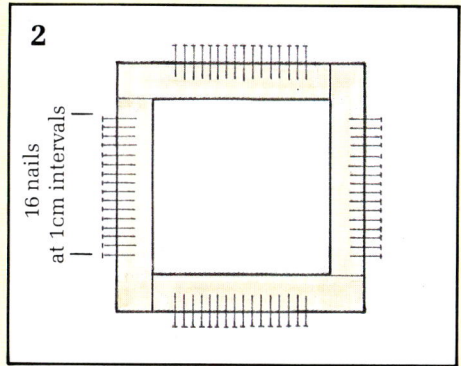

1

You will need:

Four pieces of wood 2cm x 2cm x 20cm.
68 large-headed nails (approximately 3cm long).
A hammer.
Two different coloured balls of wool.

1. Get an adult to help you make a weaving frame by nailing the four pieces of wood together to form a square.

2. Then, get an adult to help you nail in 16 nails at 1cm intervals along each side of the square.

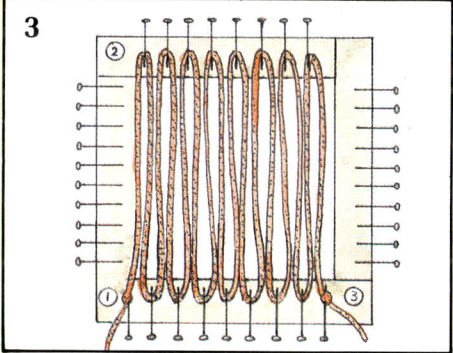

2

16 nails at 1cm intervals

3. Tie a piece of wool on the nail marked ① on the diagram and loop up and over nail ② . Continue moving the wool down and up until you reach nail ③ . Secure the wool tightly in a knot here.

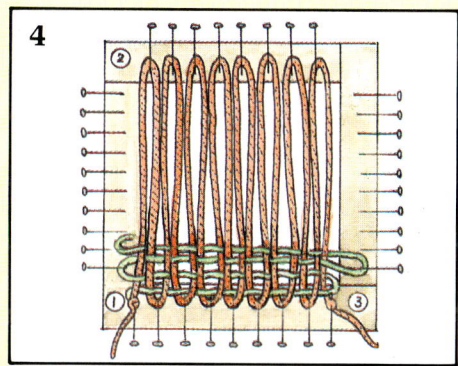

3

4. Tie a different colour wool to nail ① . Weave the thread over and under the vertical threads. When you reach nail ③ , start weaving the thread back to the left-hand side. Continue weaving horizontally over and under until you reach the top of the frame. Make sure you occasionally push the threads down, so there are no large 'gaps' in the weave.

4

Remember to secure the wool at nail ② . Your finished cloth should be similar to the picture (left).

From cloth to clothes

Most clothes we wear are shaped by cutting and sewing so that they fit our bodies. Some clothes, like *saris* and *sarongs,* are draped rather than shaped. Like the ancient Roman *togas, saris* and *sarongs* are wound round the body and fall in loose folds.

Shaped clothes are more complicated. You need several tools to sew them – like scissors, pins, needles, thread and a thimble.

Sewing by hand is the oldest method of making clothes. Prehistoric people used bone needles to sew their animal skins together, using vegetable fibre or animal sinew (muscle). Metal needles, the sort we use now, were introduced in the thirteenth century. Later, in 1790, a much easier way of sewing came along: the sewing machine, which sews faster and more evenly than any human hand. The sewing machine was invented by a London cabinet-maker called Thomas Saint.

Use a needle and thread to sew two pieces of cloth together. Then, gently pull the two pieces apart, and see how the thread holds them. It should make a zig-zig or ladder pattern.

Thomas Saint's sewing machine invented in 1790.

14

clothes pieces

1. Study a dress or jacket. How many sections make up these garments? Look for the seams where the pieces have been sewn together.

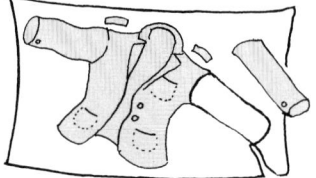

2. Draw each section smaller, but to scale, on a piece of paper, and then cut out the pieces.

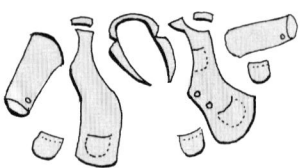

3. Shuffle the pieces around, and then try to put them back together as a dress or jacket.

4. This is only a 'flat' picture of the dress or jacket. Remember that clothes have to be shaped to fit round our bodies. Look at a proper dressmaker's pattern. The pattern pieces are difficult to recognise and have strange shapes. It is only when they are sewn together that they look like the garment.

3 Clothes and weather

Dressing for warm weather

In hot weather, clothes can help to keep you cool. They also protect your skin from the strong rays of the sun. People on the African continent and in tropical countries, who have lived in a hot climate for centuries, know the best way to dress to suit the climate. Their traditional clothes are usually loose and flowing so that they allow air to flow over the skin and cool it. These clothes cover most of the body, but cover it lightly. Loose tunics, *saris, sarongs* and also *kaftans* are worn in hot countries. *Kaftans* are long, loose garments worn by men and women in North Africa.

Most hot weather garments are made in white or some other light, bright colours. This is because lighter colours do not absorb heat as much as dark colours do. This helps keep people cooler.

Cotton is an excellent material for hot weather, because it is permeable and lets air flow through it. Synthetics, which are *not* permeable, are not so good: they can become hot and sticky to wear when temperatures are high because they do not let air reach the skin.

Find out how to wear a *sari*. If you can, get hold of a piece of real *sari* cloth. Otherwise, a small sheet will do. Walk around in your *sari*. Then describe the differences between wearing it and a school uniform.

As you know, light, loose-fitting clothes that cover most of the body are very suitable in hot countries. Yet, when people from cold countries go on their summer holidays to hot places, they usually prefer to wear shorts and bikinis. Ask

your family or friends why they do this instead of dressing more like the people who live in hot countries? Many people will say that they wear less clothes because they are tired of being wrapped up in lots of layers during the winter!

Dressing for cold weather

People have always needed clothes to help keep them warm. Clothes not only keep the cold from reaching our skins, they also stop our bodies from losing their natural heat. In ancient Greece, where it was often very cold in winter, people wore several layers of clothes – tunics, robes and cloaks – one on top of the other. People who live in very cold places today, like Finland in north-east Europe, still dress this way. The air which becomes trapped between the layers of clothes keeps them warm.

Thicker clothes act as 'barriers' against the cold. Heavy woollen garments keep out the cold air, and synthetic materials are particularly good for keeping warm because, as you already know, they are not permeable.

Today, many homes are centrally heated, so we only really need warm clothes when out of doors. Before central heating, people needed clothes to keep them warm inside their homes, as well as outside. Find a picture showing modern outdoor clothes and compare them with the picture below of indoor clothes worn in the past. Make a list of similarities and differences between them.

In the past, homes were very cold and draughty because there were often just open spaces for windows and no central heating. People wore many more clothes indoors than they do today – some even wore hats, as in this sixteenth-century picture.

4 Clothes for protection

Clothes and work

The work people do can sometimes be harmful, so they may need clothes for protection. Fire-fighters, for instance, wear flame-proof suits. Workers using road drills may wear ear-muffs to stop the noise harming their hearing.

Clothes have protected people at work for a very long time. Blacksmiths, for example, wore leather aprons to shield them from the sparks

People have worn special clothes for protection at work for many centuries. Blacksmiths wore long, thick leather aprons to protect them from the hot metal of the forges.

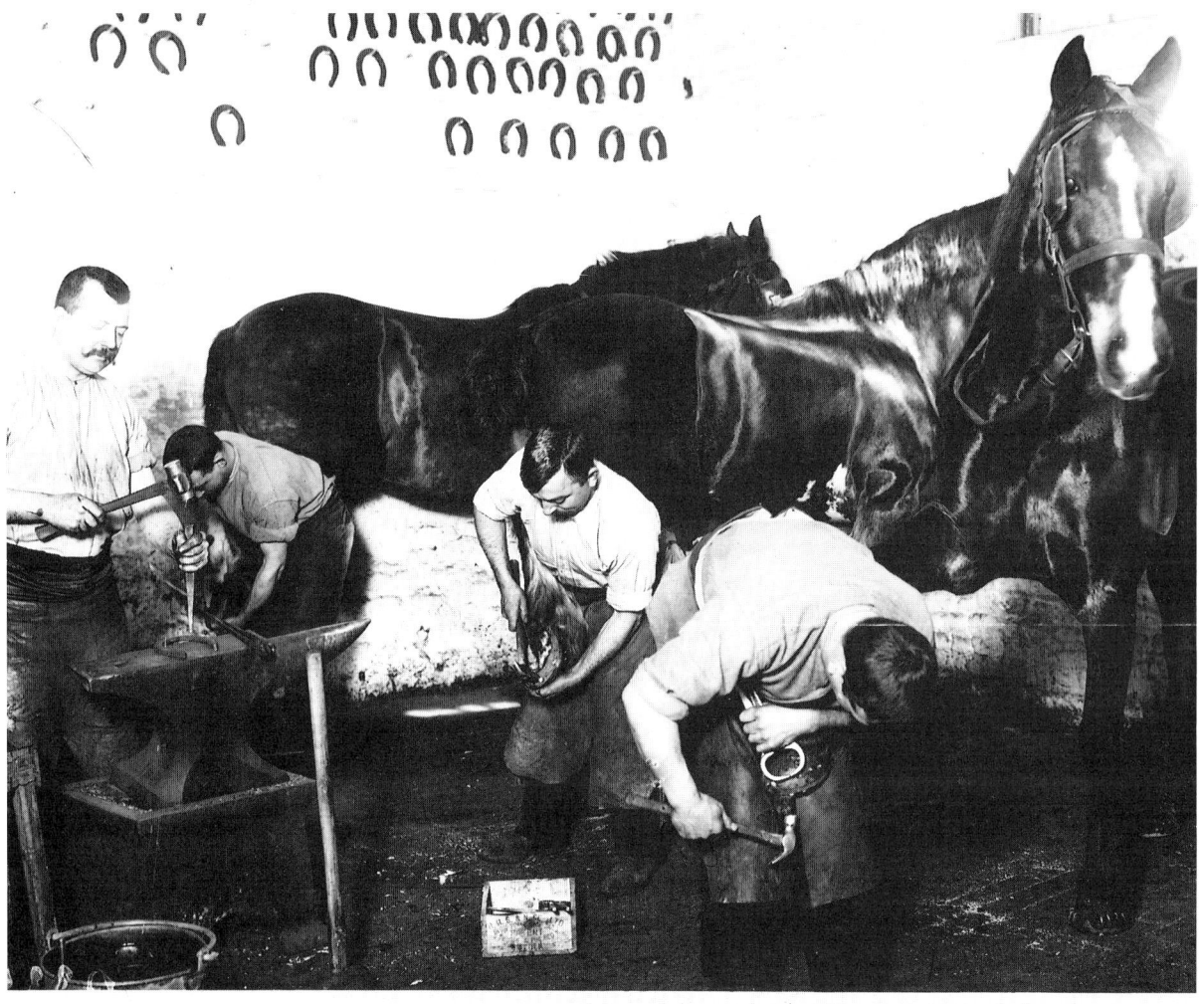

flying out of their forges, or from a horse kicking them while being shoed. Coalmen wore special hats with a long extra piece of cloth at the back, which protected their necks and heads, while carrying heavy sacks of coal on their back. Butchers wore straw hats and striped aprons and farmworkers wore wide hats or bonnets to protect themselves from the rain or sun.

Clothes for combat

Protective clothing has been important in wars and battles for many centuries. Roman soldiers wore strips of leather on their tunics to protect against sword-thrusts or blows from other heavy weapons. A thousand years ago, in Europe, knights on horseback wore 'chain mail' armour made of rings of metal. Later, from about 1350, plates of metal were used for suits of armour. Men in battle usually wore helmets to protect their heads. Look at a picture of a suit of plate armour. How was the wearer able to bend their arms at the elbow and also bend their knees?

In this century, soldiers' uniforms have been made of a dull, earth-coloured cloth called khaki and more recently, they have worn battledress coloured in browns and greens. The purpose of these twentieth-century battle-clothes has been to make the wearers blend into the landscape so that their enemies cannot see them easily.

'Camouflage' comes from a French word meaning 'disguise': modern soldiers who wear camouflage uniforms are less easy to see in the undergrowth or a forest.

Try your hand at designing one of these combat uniforms for these types of landscape:

● High, snow-covered mountain slopes
● Desert ● Forest or woodland

Below This metal suit of armour is very different from modern camouflage combat dress. The hard metal sections protected against sword-thrusts, but also allowed the wearer to move.

19

Look at workpeople in the past and now. Old pictures and postcards can show you people at work in the past. For people at work today, all you have to do is to observe them in the streets of your town: there are window cleaners, road menders, bus conductors and conductresses, postmen and postwomen, milkmen and milkwomen, traffic wardens, lorry drivers and so on. Make a chart similar to the one on this page and observe what people at work wear. Decide how their clothes suit the work they are doing.

Clothes protect people from dangers at work, but sometimes workers wear these clothes to protect other things from themselves. Find out why workers in computer rooms wear special overalls, face masks and hair coverings. What is the purpose of the sterile (germ-free) gowns and gloves worn in hospital operating theatres? Who wears them?

Above *This 1910 postcard is of a cellarman. He wears an apron and work boots for protection when carrying beer barrels.*

clothes and work

PEOPLE AT WORK	TYPES OF CLOTHES	SUITABILITY TO WORK CONDITIONS
WINDOW CLEANER	Loose, comfortable trousers. Warm jumper and sensible work boots.	Work out of doors. Safe boots for climbing ladders.
ROAD REPAIRER	Thick black overalls, fingerless gloves. Heavy steel toe-capped work boots.	Work dirty and messy. Dangerous hot tar and heavy machinery so need for overalls and protective work boots.
TRAFFIC WARDEN	Uniform of black and yellow. Thick overcoat, hat and gloves.	Uniform so they are easily recognized. Work in all weathers so need for warm coat and hat.
MILK WOMAN	Uniform coat and hat. Dark skirt and sensible low-heeled walking shoes. Fingerless gloves.	Uniform so they are easily recognized. Comfortable shoes as a great deal of walking in the job. Fingerless gloves in winter to keep hands warm, but still make it easy to carry bottles.

20

5 Sport and leisure clothes

Until about a century ago, sports and games were mainly for fun and a way for people to entertain themselves. No one thought it necessary to have special sports clothes: ordinary everyday clothes were worn.

People still play sports for fun, of course, but today, sport is a profession as well; that is, some people earn their living by playing a particular sport. Professional sportspeople need to wear clothes that help them move easily so that they can play to the best of their ability. Team sports like football, cricket or netball, need a sort of uniform for players, to show which team they belong to. And there are many sports like ice-hockey or motor-racing which can be fast and dangerous, and require clothing for protection.

All these are reasons why many sports players no longer wear ordinary clothes, but instead have special clothes for their activity.

Cricketers, for instance, wear shin pads to shield their legs and helmets to protect their

Modern sports clothes are designed for their purpose. In American football, players wear four thigh, knee and shin pads, as well as huge shoulder pads to protect themselves against hard tackling and bodychecks.

heads: they could be injured by a heavy cricket ball flying through the air. Hockey, rugby and American football are very rough games, so players wear body-padding. Swimmers wear light, smooth swimsuits or trunks to help them move faster and more easily through the water. Skiers wear goggles to protect their eyes from the wind and the glare of the snow, as well as warm ski-suits to protect them against the cold. The light clothing worn by gymnasts has to stretch easily, to give the freedom of movement they need. In motorcar or motorbike racing, crashes and fires are ever present risks, so participants wear crash helmets and flame-proof clothing.

Using history books, and the pictures on these pages, study the sports clothes of people in the past. How were tennis dresses different to those of today (see page 6). Were football strips very different? How many sports can you think of where players wear:

- loose shorts
- helmets
- short skirts
- gloves

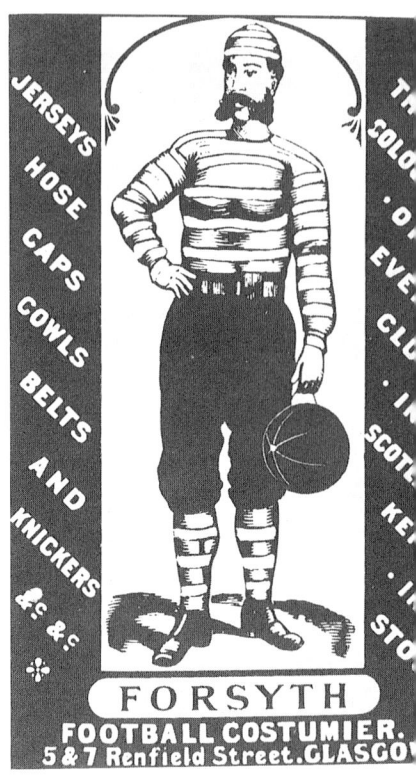

Above An 1876 advertisement for football kits. Old advertisements provide excellent and amusing clues to clothes in the past.

Left Old photographs can tell us a great deal about clothes in the past. Football team strips in the early 1930s were very different from those of today, as this picture shows. What are the main differences between these early strips, compared with today's?

In Britain, seaside holidays first became popular about two centuries ago, and swimming in the sea later became an enjoyable part of these holidays. However, men and women were accustomed to covering themselves up in lots of clothes, especially in the late nineteenth century. So, men and women wore very elaborate swimsuits which covered up their legs. It was also fashionable to use a bathing machine at the seaside. This was a small hut on wheels, which was pulled into the sea by a horse. Inside, bathers would change into their bathing suits and creep quickly into the sea!

Look at the picture on the right. Why do you think the people in Victorian Britain wore such elaborate costumes? How were these costumes similar to, and how were they different from, the clothes they wore at home? In what way are they different to modern swimwear?

Far below Hastings Beach, Sussex in 1901, showing bathing machines for hire. *Inset* A family of bathers from the same period.

23

6 Clothes and people

Clothes as a disguise

Very few people have 'perfect' figures. People often feel they are taller than they want to be or shorter. Clothes have always been very useful in this respect. In the eighteenth century, very short women sometimes wore platforms on their shoes to make themselves look taller. These platforms could be up to half a metre high, but because skirts reached down to the ground, no one saw them. At about the same time, men with very thin legs used to wear padding underneath their long hose, or stockings, to make their calves look fuller. One Queen of England, Anne Boleyn, second wife of Henry VIII, had six fingers on one hand, so she started a fashion for wearing special 'indoor' gloves: this enabled her to hide the defect.

Today, people who are very short can still wear high-heeled shoes if they feel it is important to appear taller. People with fuller figures can wear vertical (up and down) stripes in their clothes, or wear darker colours: this way, they can appear slimmer. Conversely, thin people can make themselves look 'wider' by wearing horizontal (side to side) stripes or lighter colours.

The picture shows you a slimmer person. Suppose you were choosing a wardrobe of clothes for a larger person and a slimmer person to take on a summer holiday. What would you choose?

What clothes say about you

Clothes can give out different signals about the people who wear them. For instance, you can easily recognize a policeman or policewoman or

Clothes can act as a disguise – dark clothes can make you look slimmer, vertical stripes can make you look taller and horizontal stripes can make you appear wider.

a nurse by their uniforms. You can also recognize nuns or monks by their long, simple robes which no one else wears today.

Have you ever been a bridesmaid or a page-boy at a wedding? The special clothes you wore 'told' everyone who saw you that day what you were doing. And, of course, everyone can identify a bride when she wears her special wedding dress and head-dress. This is because no one wears wedding clothes *except* for a wedding.

Many people like to follow fashion. They take an interest in the latest styles, probably read fashion magazines and buy new clothes quite often. If you see people wearing new fashions, this could tell you that they are interested in clothes in general, and also in their own appearance.

What do you think are the advantages of following fashion? What are the disadvantages? Discuss with your friends whether or not they think it is good to be fashionable. After all, lots of people just ignore fashions and wear what they like.

Above Many teenagers think it is important to be fashionable, but what is fashionable one year is 'old-fashioned' the next.

Left These bridesmaids are wearing special clothes for just one day. 'Dressing up' is often part of an important occasion.

7 Clothes in history

As you know from the previous pages, clothes can 'talk'. One of the things they tell about people is the time in which they lived. In the early 1940s during the Second World War (1939–1945), women's fashions had a 'military' look about them. Jacket shoulders were very wide, and were usually padded. The skirts were narrow and clothes were made in dark colours. The narrow line of the clothes was due to the fact that less material was used in such styles. This was important when rationing was introduced in the war due to a shortage of material. Such wartime clothes became known as 'utility clothes', as they were practical and unfrivolous.

After the war was over in 1945, there was a

Far left Before the 1920s, women always wore their dresses long. This 1920s cocktail dress shows how clothes had finally become more daring.

Left In the 1930s, clothes became more formal and tailored. A hat was essential for men, as well as women, to 'finish off' an outfit.

marvellous feeling of freedom. Clothes reflected this, too. In 1947, Christian Dior, a French fashion designer, brought out his 'New Look'. The 'Look' featured brighter colours to reflect the happier post-war times people looked forward to. It also included very full skirts which used lots of material. This was not the first, or the last time, that the circumstances in which people lived affected how they dressed.

Ask someone at home to tell you when a film made in the 1930s, 1940s or 1950s, is going to be shown on television. But, make sure they do not tell you the exact decade the film was made. Study pictures of men's and women's clothing from these three decades. Then watch the film and, from the clothes the actors and actresses are wearing, work out in which decade the film was made. You can also do the same with costume dramas such as 'David Copperfield' or 'Oliver Twist'.

Far left During the years of the Second World War (1939–1945), clothes took on a military look, with tight-fitting skirts and jackets. This was partly due to a shortage of material available to make clothes.

Left After the Second World War, dresses in the 1950s became much more gathered and full. This reflected the carefree attitudes of the time.

Suppose you lived in Roman Britain

After the Romans invaded and occupied most of Britain in AD 43, they brought with them their own way of life. Some Britons began to live in towns that were just like those in other parts of the vast Roman Empire. These Britons also wore Roman clothes.

Rich, important men wore long draped *togas*. Rich older boys also wore *togas*. These had a purple stripe along the edge until they were sixteen years old: after that, the boys' *togas* were white. The women and girls wore long, full tunics which hung in graceful folds.

Not everyone was rich, of course. Poorer men living in Roman British towns or country villas wore short tunics with an extra cloak called a *penula* in cold weather. Ordinary women wore tunics, just like the rich women, but the cloth was not nearly so fine, silky or expensive.

*Typical dress worn in Roman times. **Left to right:** a poor Roman man and boy; a rich Roman woman in a long tunic of fine material; a rich Roman man in a long draped toga.*

ROMAN DRESS AD43 ~ AD 476

Look at the drawings on page 28, of Roman dress. Which of their garments are still being worn today? Which are not being generally worn? What is the chief difference between the traditional dress of Roman men, and of modern men today?

Study the drawing of a *toga*. Then, use a sheet to make one for yourself. Compare this with the *sari*. Are they quite similar?

Suppose you lived in a castle

In the four centuries when the Romans ruled in Britain, the country was relatively orderly and peaceful. However, after the Romans left, in about AD 476, there followed a long period of unrest. There were many outlaws living in the forests, and many robbers waiting to attack travellers on the roads. In the eleventh and twelfth centuries, people began to band together in feudal

Typical dress worn in Norman times. **Left to right:** *a serf dressed in thick, coarse cloth; a Norman baron's wife; a poor boy; a Norman baron in a woollen tunic trimmed with fur, and a thick cape.*

NORMAN DRESS 1066~1154

29

communities which were protected by powerful barons. This was a safer way of life, but unfortunately, the barons who had private armies, were in the habit of making war with each other. To protect themselves from their rivals, barons and their families lived in castles with strong stone walls and high battlements. These castles were safer to live in, but they were very cold and dark. They were also damp, despite the fires burning in some of the rooms. The stone staircases and passageways were very draughty.

Clothes helped give people who lived in castles some warmth and comfort. Men wore woollen tunics, sometimes one on top of the other, and women wore long tunic dresses. Under their dresses, women wore bodices with long, tight-fitting sleeves and, like the men, sometimes wore fur trimmings and high collars. Boys and girls usually dressed in the same styles as adults, although in plainer materials. Because of the way they lived, they wore far more clothes indoors than we do today.

Visit a stone building, perhaps an old church or castle, in your area. Imagine living there. How is it different from your own home? Look at paintings of the eleventh and twelfth century people. How many garments are they wearing? If you lived in a castle, what kind of clothes would you wear: choose from your own wardrobe.

A portrait of a wealthy family in the early seventeenth century. Notice the huge collars, or ruffs, and the lace on the child's dress at the front of the picture.

Suppose you lived in the seventeenth century

In the seventeenth century, wealthy people, like merchants and nobles, wore colourful, fussy clothes. Men and boys wore huge ruffs, made of lace, as this was very popular during the period. Sleeves had slashes, or cuts, to show the shirts underneath. Dresses had tight waists and full skirts. Hats were lavishly decorated with feathers and clothes often has masses of ribbons and frills. By wearing such clothes, people were showing off their wealth and importance.

The Puritans, who were very religious Christians, did not approve of such lavish dressing. They believed vanity, and the love of pleasure and comfort were sinful. These ideas were reflected in the way the Puritans dressed. Their clothes were plain and unadorned, as they admired simplicity. The colours were unpretentious: black, brown, white. Puritans did not wear imported silks, because they thought them ostentatious. Of course, poorer people at the time, dressed similarly to Puritans. However, for them it was not out of choice, but because they could not afford the finery and lace.

Even so, the Puritans were still wearing clothes that could be recognized as 'seventeenth century style'. If you look back to the page 28 describing clothes worn in ancient Rome, you will see that clothes had evolved a great deal over the centuries from the simple tunics. The next section shows how some of these changes took place.

Lace patterns

1. Find two different pieces of lace (perhaps on a handkerchief and net curtain).

2. Study the pattern of the lace and make a drawing of each of the designs on a piece of paper.

3. Draw your own lace design or make a list of clothes or articles in your home which have lace on them.

17th century Dress

A seventeenth-century nobleman and a puritan woman. While many of the clothes in the seventeenth century were flamboyant and highly decorated, the puritans preferred very plain, simple clothes of sombre browns and black.

8 Looking at clothes

Trousers and shirts

We often think of trousers as traditional clothing for men and boys, even though women and girls wear them a great deal today. It was not always so. For many centuries, it was traditional for men as well as women to wear gowns and loose garments with skirts. The gradual change to trousers began about 1,500 years ago. At that time, in the later days of the Roman Empire, the soldiers guarding the borders against attack by barbarians, such as Goths and Huns, began to copy the long woollen trousers worn by their enemies. The Romans had long believed that trousers were vulgar and ugly, but as they soon discovered, they were warm and comfortable.

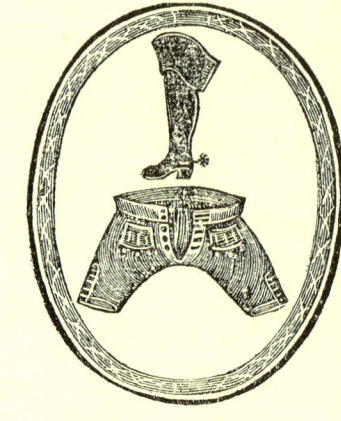

James Potter,
Leather - Breeches Make

At the Sign of the Boot *and* Breec
within Three Doors of Aldgate
the Left Hand Side of the Way
Shoemaker-Row.

M Aketh and Selleth all Sort
Leather-Breeches, by Wl
fale and Retail, at Reafonable R.
Likewife Buck and Doe Skins
all Sorts of Leather for Breecl

Printed at the Old Katherine-Wheel without Bifho

Above An early eighteenth-century clothes advertisement. Large signs (like the one at the top of the picture) of the shop's goods were hung outside, as not many people could read. Leather breeches were worn by working men during this period.

Left Short breeches and hose (thick stockings) were very popular in the late sixteenth and seventeenth centuries, as this painting shows.

Men have worn some form of leg-covering ever since. In medieval times, they covered their legs with cloth tied round with garters, or with stocking-like hose and breeches. Then, modern trousers arrived at the start of the nineteenth century, when men began to copy the loose, baggy trousers worn by the 'sans-culottes', who were the poor Parisians of the French Revolution in 1789.

'Oxford bags' as these trousers were called, became fashionable in the 1920s. Modern long trousers became fashionable at the start of the nineteenth century, following the style of the loose, baggy trousers worn by poor Parisians at the time of the French Revolution (1789).

Meanwhile, tunics – once worn by the ancient Greeks and Romans – had changed their form. First, tunics were tucked in at the waist. Then, they were given sleeves and collars, and finally cravats (neck scarves) and ties. So, over a long period of time, the ancient tunic evolved into the shirt of today.

Why do you think that the wearing of trousers suited the way of life of the Goths and the Huns? Look at the drawing of the man in a tunic on page 28. What needs to be done to the tunic to make it into a shirt? What must be added to it? How must it be altered at the front?

The traditional tunic of ancient Rome gradually evolved into the modern shirt. This picture, of late seventeenth-century dress, shows that the design of the shirt was still quite loose during this period, and had a cravat rather than a tie.

Skirts and dresses

After men began wearing trousers, women went on wearing dresses and skirts. For many centuries, women's dresses were basically long, loose tunics, sometimes worn with a belt. Then, in about 1400, tunics were given waists, and skirts became very full. As time went on, it became fashionable for women to wear exceedingly full and wide skirts. These often needed many petticoats or special structures to hold them up. In the sixteenth century, women often wore a large hooped frame called a farthingale. In the nineteenth century, there were crinolines first and later bustles, which were frames that pushed out the skirt. Crinolines made the skirt 'stick out' all round, while bustles made only the back of the skirt full.

Above *An example of an early dress from the Iron Age (400 BC to AD 43). This long tunic was simply gathered at the waist with a piece of string or cord.*

making a crinoline frame

You will need:
Pipe cleaners.
'Sindy'-type doll, or cardboard kitchen roll tube.
Strong glue (not 'superglue').
Sticky tape.
Ribbon or bias binding.
Ruler.
Circle of material 32cm in diameter.

1. Make six graduated hoops out of the pipe cleaners, starting with a diameter of 6cm, then 8cm, 10cm, 12cm, 14cm and 16cm. With the larger hoops, you will need to join more than one pipe cleaner together with tape.

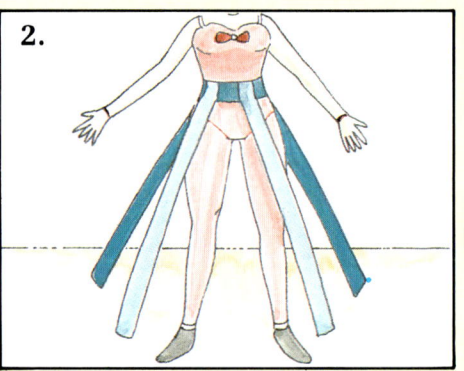

2. Take the doll and glue a circle of ribbon around the waist to act as a waistband. Then cut four pieces of ribbon, 16cm long. Stick these around the circle of ribbon at regular intervals.

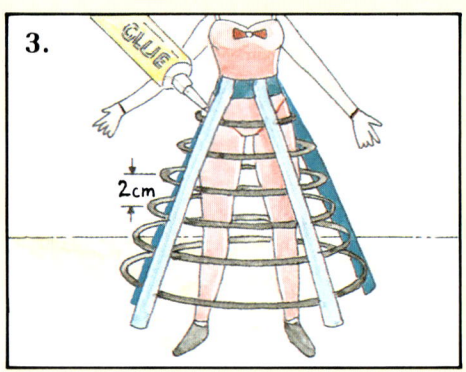

3. Take the smallest of the hoops and push it underneath the four ribbons. Position as near to the top as you can and glue into place. Take the next size hoop and position that about 2cm below the last hoop, and so on.

4. When the glue has dried take a circle of material (you can decorate with lace or bows if you want). Cut a slit of 5cm in the middle of the circle and slip over the doll's head onto the crinoline frame. This will give you an idea of how a real crinoline worked.

NOTE: The cardboard kitchen tube can be used instead of a doll. Just attach the circle of ribbon 3cm down the tube and continue as above.

Women wore these clothes because they were generally thought of be the proper, feminine type of dress, but they were not very comfortable or practical. Imagine you are wearing a crinoline. What problems would you find in getting on a bus, driving a car, walking upstairs, playing sports or going through a doorway? Look at the picture of Victorian women on these pages to help you. Clothes did not become comfortable for women until about seventy years ago, when women gained new freedoms and equality, including the right to vote in elections. Women expressed their freedom in their dress. Skirts became short for the first time after 1920, and from this time women began to wear trousers and shorts.

Above An original court dress of the 1740s, made of fine silk with hand embroidery. Its wide, yet flat sideways appearance is gained by wearing paniers (round basket-like supports) on each hip, which were hinged so they could be folded for travelling.

OUR MUTUAL FRIEND ADVERTISER.

SANSFLECTUM CRINOLINES.

Puffed Horse-hair Jupon
(*Registered*).

25s., 30s., and 33s. 6d.

☞ Admirably adapted for the Promenade, having a decided train.' — *English-woman's Domestic Magazine.*

An amusing work on Crino line gratis and post-free.

The Patent Ondina or Waved Jupon.

18s. 6d., 21s., and 26s. 6d.

' Allows the dress to fall in graceful folds.'— *Morning Post.*

Illustrations of Jupons gratis and post-free.

Left A Victorian advertisement showing the different types of crinoline frames available.

Jackets and coats

For a very long time, people wore cloaks out of doors for extra warmth in cold weather. Cloaks are still worn today in some parts of the world, though now, most people prefer coats.

Coats first became popular in Britain after King Charles II came to the throne in 1660. He started a new fashion by wearing a long 'Persian' coat with wide turned-back sleeves and buttons down the front. At first, the new coat had no collar: all the space round the neck was taken up by a large cravat or scarf.

By the eighteenth century, though, coats were given collars and revers (the turned-back edge at the front of a coat). A shortened version of the 'Persian' coat eventually became what we call a jacket, and by the nineteenth century, on both jackets and coats, collar and revers were attached to each other. There is a small nick, or cut, on modern jackets and coats to show where they were joined.

Look at old pictures and postcards and see how many people in them are wearing cloaks. Also, note how many wear coats with small cloaks attached to them. This was a popular fashion in the nineteenth century.

AboveThis Edwardian (1901–1910) coat looks much more like the modern coats of today. The collar and revers are joined to one another and there is a small 'v'-shaped cut to show where they join.

Left This early sixteenth-century jacket has no collar or revers.

Hats

Hats and head coverings have been given more shapes than any other piece of clothing. This is because hats do not need to fit the shape of the body: they just 'sit' on the head and take almost any shape – tall, wide, round, or flat.

Nearly three thousand years ago, kings in Assyria in the Middle East, wore hats shaped like tall cones. Except for the fact that they had no brims, these were not very different from the tall hats worn in the seventeenth century (see page 31) or the 'stove-pipe' top hats of a hundred years ago. So, hats in this shape are very old indeed, and are still worn today.

For a long time, at least until some fifty years ago, it was thought proper and correct for people to wear hats out of doors and sometimes indoors as well. Today, people still wear hats on formal occasions, such as weddings, and a new fashion for hats has spread among young people. Very young babies wear hats in the sun to protect them from the heat, and in the winter woolly hats to keep them warm. Many other people, however, rarely, or never, wear hats. One reason is that clothes generally have become less formal in the last forty years. Hats can be very formal, and do not usually go with informal clothes like jeans, tee-shirts or sweatshirts.

In the street of your town, look at the hats people are wearing. Make quick drawings of the shapes. Why do you think they are wearing them? Because they are fashionable? Because they are warm or because they are wearing formal clothes, and the hats 'finish off' their outfits? How many other reasons can you think of?

Look at the hats people wear at the Ascot races on television. It is a tradition, for women especially, to wear unusual hats on this day.

Above Up until the mid-twentieth century, hats were worn to 'finish off' an outfit. Although out-of-fashion until quite recently, hats are now making a comeback as everyday wear.

Clothes for children

Until two centuries ago, children were dressed like small adults – girls in tight-waisted dresses just like their mothers, and boys in doublet, hose and breeches like their fathers. Clothes for children began to change in about 1770. Around this time, the ideas of Jean-Jacques Rousseau, the Swiss-French philosopher were becoming popular. Rousseau believed children were born good and pure and should be given as much freedom as possible to enjoy and develop their goodness. This made childhood a special part of life, free from the harsh, corrupt world of adults. The new way of dressing children reflected these ideas of freedom and innocence and children's clothes became more comfortable.

Girls began to wear loose dresses and boys, soft shirts and comfortable trousers. Later on, very young boys and girls were dressed the same, in loose, light smocks. About ninety years ago, both used to wear sailor suits, which were probably the most popular fashion there has ever been for children.

Above This painting of 1636, shows how the children of rich parents used to be dressed as 'miniature adults'.

Right Can you imagine your younger sister or brother wearing a hat like this! Since the 1770s clothes had become looser and more comfortable, but this dress of 1904 still looks difficult to play in.
Inset As you can see from the picture of this little girl of the 1980s, clothes are colourful, comfortable and easy to keep clean.

Left This photograph taken in 1901 shows that children's clothes had become plainer, although they still look very smart.

Children have worn special clothes ever since. The styles have, of course, changed a great deal, but today the most important thing about children's clothes is still the same as it was in Rousseau's day: that they should give freedom of movement and be comfortable to wear.

Find pictures of children, and of men and women in the clothes they wore in the early eighteenth century. Books in your local library should have these pictures. Then, compare the clothes piece by piece – a woman's dress with a girl's dress; men's trousers with boy's trousers and so on. Note the similarities between them.

Do you have any photographs of yourself when you were younger? If so, compare the clothes you wore then with pictures of children of a similar age in the nineteenth century. Children in the past may look overdressed to you, because ideas of what is comfortable have changed, just as materials and styles have changed. Would you like to dress in the 'comfortable' clothes children wore in the past? Discuss this with friends.

Try your hand at clothes designing for children, and make them comfortable and easy to wear.

Design some clothes for yourself and your friends. Remember to keep in mind the type of fabrics you might use. Would you choose natural materials or synthetic materials?

9 A local clothes project

Eighty or ninety years ago, the town or village where you live looked quite different from the way it looks today. There was little or no motor traffic, and there were no big supermarkets. Instead, shops were small and people shopping there were served from behind long counters.

Men who worked in shops usually wore suits with a waistcoat, shirt and stiff collar. Women wore long dresses or skirts and blouses. Even in hot weather, shop assistants were very 'covered up' in their high-necked shirts and long sleeves.

Shoppers also looked different eighty or ninety years ago. Women shoppers wore long dresses with wide skirts, maybe with a shawl covering their shoulders, and a large hat. Often, they wore boots buttoned to the ankle, for it was thought immodest to show your ankles or lower leg.

Go to your local library for pictures of your town or village as it was at the beginning of this century. Look at the people shown in the street scene. Choose one person from a picture and analyse what he or she is wearing. Would you like to dress like this today? How many of the clothes in the picture are still being worn? How many people in working clothes does the picture show. How are their clothes suited to the work they do? Do you recognize any of the shops?

Can you locate a clothing shop which was trading in your town around the year 1900? Your local history society could help you. They might help you find copies of old local newspapers. Look at any clothes shop advertisements to see what the shop sold.

Find some old clothes' shop advertisements to help you with your project. You can often find old newspapers at jumble sales.

NICHOLSON'S
NEW COSTUMES AND MANTLES
AT WHOLESALE CITY PRICES.

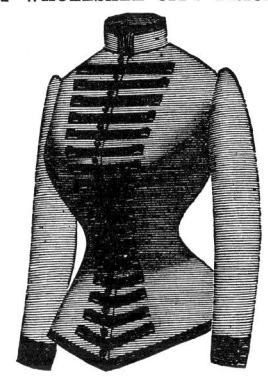

UHLAN,
in firm Stockinette, tailor-made, all sizes, 8s. 11d.
Illustrated Catalogues Free. Established 50 years.
NOVELTIES IN DRESS FABRICS, from 6d. to 2s. per yard.
NEW SILKS, PLUSHES, VELVETS, &c.

NICHOLSON & CO.,
50 to 54, ST. PAUL'S CHURCHYARD, LONDON.

SWANBILL CORSETS
(REGISTERED).

THIRD TYPE OF FIGURE.
WHITE .. 21s. 0d.
BLACK .. 25s. 6d.

A specially constructed Belt Corset for Ladies inclined to embonpoint.

Corset and Belt - Key, Illustrated by Twelve Types of Figure, sent post-free.

Send Size of Waist, with P.O.O., on Sloane-street.

ADDLEY BOURNE,
Ladies' Warehouse,
174, SLOANE - STREET,
BELGRAVIA
(late of Piccadilly).

TRADE-MARKS.

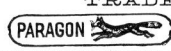

PARAGON   LOCK RIB

IN BUYING AN UMBRELLA see that one of the above Trade-Marks is on the Frame. These Frames, of sterling quality, are manufactured only by SAMUEL FOX and CO., Limited, whose Frames have given perfect satisfaction for the last thirty-five years. To be had of all respectable Umbrella Dealers.

10 Clothes in the future

From time to time, clothes designers like to make predictions about the sort of clothes people might wear in the future. Some of their ideas are both interesting and amusing as well as practical. One designer thought up a very novel type of dress: it had a back which could be inflated to provide the wearer with a seat! Another designed a 'Body Bubble', a vinyl garment with inflatable sections: blow up all the sections and you would be inside a ball, and could roll, bounce or float around. There were clothes with metal parts – aluminium collars, or metal squares joined by leather – and

Nobody knows what our clothes in the future will be like. Some people think they will be influenced by space exploration. Can you imagine wearing clothes in the twenty-first century like the ones worn in the musical Starlight Express?

an 'Osmosis Helmet' with a built-in power pack that could massage your head or play soothing music in your ears.

Draw or paint a picture of a person in 'futuristic' clothes. What material would you choose? Disposable clothes, made of paper fabrics have been designed quite recently. What would be the advantages of such clothes.

Remember that future fashion may be influenced by events – like modern space exploration. It can also be influenced by the past and the clothes worn then. It would also help if you thought about what you have discovered in this book about the way clothes have developed from one time in history to the next.

Places to visit

Your local museum might have a section or special exhibition on clothes in history, or your local library may be able to supply some of the books mentioned on page 46. There are also more specialized clothes museums. Listed below are some of the museums specializing in, or featuring, clothes through the ages.

Armagh County Museum, The Mall East, Armagh, Northern Ireland.
Armley Mills, Museum of Leeds, Canal, Armley, Leeds.
Carlisle Museum and Art Gallery, Tullie House, Castle Street, Carlisle.
Bexhill Manor Costume Museum, Bexhill, East Sussex.
Devonshire Collection of Period Clothes, Bogan House, 42 High Street, Totnes, Devon.
Dre-Fach Felindre, Museum of the Woollen Industry, Dre-Fach Felindre, near Newcastle Emlyn, Dyfed, Wales.

The Gallery of English Costume, Platt Hall, Platt Fields, Rusholme, Manchester.

Glencoe and North Lorn Folk Museum, Glencoe, Scotland.

Hawick Museum and Art Gallery, Wilton Lodge Park, Hawick, Scotland.

Museum of Costume, Assembly Rooms, Bath, Avon.

The Museum of Costume and Textiles, 51 Castlegate, Nottingham.

The Museum of Mankind, 6 Burlington Gardens, London W1X 2EZ.

The Old House Museum, Cunningham Place, Bakewell, Derbyshire.

Shambellie House Museum of Costume, New Abbey, Dunfries, Scotland.

The Victoria and Albert Museum, Cromwell Road, South Kensington, London, SW7 2RL.

Wygston's House, Museum of Costume, Applegate, Leicester.

Further reading

Broughton, W., *Learnabout Crochet* (Ladybird, 1975)

Cooke, J., *Costumes and Clothes* (Wayland, 1986)

Crommelin, J., *The Pegasus Book of Fabric Crafts* (Dobson, 1970)

Dicks, P., *Sports Clothes* (Wayland, 1987)

Lansdell, A., *Occupational Costumes* (Shire, 1977)

Lewis, B. R., *Just Look at . . . Clothes* (Macdonald, 1986)

Moss, M., *Clothes in Cold Weather* (Wayland, 1988)

Moss, M., *Clothes in Hot Weather* (Wayland, 1988)

Selbie, R., *The Anatomy of Costume* (Bell & Hyman, 1982)

Sewell, C., *Clothes in History* (Wayland, 1983)

Sichel, M., *Costume Reference Library* (Batsford, 1982). (This series contains many books on the costumes of different periods in history)

Williams-Mitchell, C., *Dressed for the Job* (Blandford Press, 1982)

Yarwood, D., *Costumes of the Western World* (Lutterworth Press, 1980)

Glossary

Artificial   Not natural.

Bathing machine   A bathing hut on wheels in which people can change into swimming costumes without being seen.

Bodice   A garment worn by women, similar to a vest; or just the upper part of a woman's dress.

Breeches   A type of trousers usually reaching to the knee.

Cellulose   Substance forming the solid parts of plants.

Civilization   The highly developed life of a particular people, including their science, art and writing.

Cocoons   Silky case spun by larvae, especially silkworm larvae, to protect themselves.

Culture   Way of life, or customs.

Decade   A period of ten years.

Distaff   A metre-long stick, split at the top for winding wool and other thread before hand-spinning.

Doublet   A short jacket worn by men stretching from the neck to the tops of the legs.

Equality   Men and women having the same opportunities in life, and the same responsibilities and duties.

Feudal communities   Groups ruled by a baron to whom the people swore to be loyal if war arose.

French Revolution   An uprising against King Louis XVI in France in 1789.

Ostentatious   Showing off wealth or fine clothes and jewels.

Polymers   Mixtures of chemicals.

Prehistoric   Before the time when historical records were kept.

Rationing   To share out a fixed amount to one person. Rationing was often put into practise for food and clothing during the Second World War (1939–1945).

Synthetics   Materials made by mixing chemicals, and then spinning the mixture into thread for weaving.

Thimble   A small metal bell-shaped covering to protect one or two fingertips while sewing.

Unpretentious   Modest, quiet, without pride.

'Utility clothes'   Plain, clothes, made from as little material as possible, worn during the Second World War.

Vanity   To be proud of yourself, and boastful about your achievements or appearance.

Index

Picture Ackowledgements
The publishers would like to thank the following for supplying pictures: The Billie Love Collection 40 (below); BBC Hulton Picture Library 6, 12 (above), 14, 18, 23 (main picture), 24 (above), 26 (left), 27 (left and right), 28 (below), 41 (main picture), 35 (below); BPCC/Aldus Archive 4, 8 (below), 21, 26 (right), 35 (above), 38 (above), 39 (above); Camera Press 25 (above); E.T. Archive 17; David Evans 25 (below); The Hutchison Library 5, 16 (both), 19 (above), 20 (below); Martin Offer 41 (inset); Peter Newark's Western Americana 10 (below), 22 (above); Popperfoto 23 (inset), 33, 34; TOPHAM 22 (below), 24 (below), 37 (above), 44. The remaining pictures are from the Wayland Picture Library.